HIRED MUSICIAN

A GUIDE TO GETTING AND KEEPING GIGS

Mat Maxwell and Seth Costner

hired musician

noun. A musician who is paid to perform with an artist or band.

—

CONTENTS

Prelude..................................6

1. Getting Gigs........................9

2. Keeping Gigs.....................18

3. Music...............................26

4. Money..............................33

5. Mindset............................43

6. Myths...............................53

7. Musings............................64

Encore................................86

Resource List......................88

Index..................................90

About the Authors...............91

Acknowledgements.............92

PRELUDE

This book is a collection of info, tips, and opinions from two dudes who decided to jump headfirst into becoming what's colloquially known as "sidemen" or "hired guns" in the music industry. Our goal is to help readers become more hirable and desirable to potential employers.

Whom or what does a hired musician support? Well, the band, but ultimately the biggest part of that is giving the boss, bandleader, or person doing the hiring what they want. The boss might be a lead singer, producer, or an engineer. Relationally, they could be a complete stranger or even a friend or acquaintance. Whatever the case, the boss' vision and leadership should be supported by strong team members. Team members must be able to deliver what that person needs in terms of music and beyond. This book deals mostly with the beyond – things like the "hang" or "vibe." You may hear these words a lot, but exactly what do they mean? Can you improve your "hang" or "vibe," and if so, how? We'll delve into demystifying these concepts and shed some light on many other aspects of being a hired musician – especially some of the more ambiguous ones like burnout, tour etiquette, pay negotiation, and not burning bridges.

In addition to spending most of our lives as full-time musicians, we've dedicated many hours to researching various fields including psychology, human relations, business, and communication, which strongly influenced the information in this survival guide. Between the two of us, we've probably played almost every type of gig under the sun, from the shoe section at a local department store in Alabama all the way to Madison Square Garden. With that in mind, we wrote this book for the musicians who aspire to play on the biggest stages and in the best studios. But it is also for the ones who want to be part of a regional wedding band, land a cruise ship gig, or just play at their local bar.

Bear in mind that in this industry, we deal with some elements of getting gigs that are totally out of our control. One of those elements is that your work is going to involve other humans to some degree, and if you're looking for a job where you don't have to deal with people, you're going to be disappointed. Our value isn't just in our skills – it's also in how well we work with others.

We'd like to add that each musician's journey might look a little different, and we certainly don't know everything about every situation. Your path might even be vastly different from either of ours, but we believe you can benefit greatly from some of the ideas in this book. We'll state some universal truths, as well as some tips and opinions we've learned and adopted along the way. Ultimately though, it is colored by our experiences only. This is exactly why we went to great lengths to gain insight into how the music business operates as a whole. Some of the tips we give are not going to be applicable to every scenario – one size doesn't fit all. Experience will always be the greatest teacher, but both of us wish we had been a little more prepared and aware of all the ins and outs of being a hired musician from the jump.

What we hope to achieve in writing this book is to provide truths and insight that can help you on your way, save you some time and energy, and force you into moments of self-reflection so you can be the best version of yourself. This will enable you to be more employable. We hope that this labor of love will help you in all of these aspects. May it aid you in your quest for work in the industry.

ALWAYS

PUT IN THE

WORK.

IT'LL ALWAYS BE

WORTH IT.

CHAPTER 1: GETTING GIGS

So you made it past the intro. Nice! Now let's get right to it and jump headfirst into the dos and don'ts of getting gigs. Some of them may be obvious to you, while others may not.

—

Hone Your Craft - While mastery of your instrument is a lifelong journey, there are some basic skills you need to have before you ever step foot on stage. First and foremost, you have to be able to play well. So if you haven't already honed your craft, put this book down for a second and go practice. Alright, now that you're ready...

Show Up - This sounds funny and should be obvious, but some people don't even make it this far. If you agree to be somewhere, be there. Have a stomach ache? Push through. In a coma? Wake up! We're obviously being facetious with the second one, but you get the point. If you won't do it, someone else will. Also, learn to keep a good calendar and be as organized as you can. You'll inevitably make a mistake – we're all human – but do the best you can to ensure that you don't ever leave anyone hanging. They won't soon forget if you do.

Show Up on Time - We've all heard the expression "early is on time, on time is late, late is unforgivable." Just stick with that and you'll be good. Showing up on time is respectful to the person who hired you and to the other musicians. The last thing you need is to be fighting any added awkwardness because you planned poorly.

Show Up Prepared - This could mean a number of different things depending on the situation, like memorization, sight-reading skills, ability to improvise, or having the right gear. Do what you gotta do to deliver the goods! Most of us have stayed up all night studying for a test, playing video games, or hanging with friends, so why wouldn't you do the same to be prepared for a performance or a session? You'll almost never look back on a gig and say to yourself, "I wish I would have practiced less for that job." Always put in the work. It'll always be worth it.

Practice Good Hygiene - You're going to be in close proximity to your co-workers, and taking care of yourself in this department is a basic matter of respect for yourself and others. Good hygiene is going to keep you healthy and working. It also has the added psychological benefit of making you feel better; and if you feel better, you will perform better.

Dress for the Job - Unless it's expressly stated otherwise, you can't go wrong with simple, all-black attire. In some situations, bands will want you to wear something specific or even flashy. It never hurts to ask if you're unsure. If you can, try to find some videos to see what musicians in your specific genre or role are wearing. Extra diligence in this area can go a long way in the entertainment industry.

Be Positive - A good attitude is helpful for getting and keeping gigs. Heck, why not smile as much as you can? It can't hurt and, in fact, it can be contagious. Ever been around someone who just brings the mood of the room down? It makes for an awful work environment and can start to impact your overall happiness in life.

Treat Everyone Well - You never know who could be a potential employer or recommend you to an employer. Someone with undeniable talent who is impossible to be around will not have the same success as a lesser player who treats everyone well. Good character is an essential part of this business.

Be Coachable - There is always room for growth, and you will definitely be coached at some point. Don't take offense to feedback or even hard critique – inevitably you will have to swallow your pride and do what you're asked to do even if you don't fully agree with it. That critique may come from the artist or band for whom you're working, the musical director, or even that overly abrasive sound guy (ha!). We all have strengths and weaknesses, and you should be okay with someone pointing out an area that needs improvement. At the end of the day, the performance AND your career are going to flourish as a result of your humility. It's definitely not a fun thing to do, but try to find and face your flaws. We all have blind spots, so make efforts to identify and improve them.

Don't Be Afraid to Say Yes - Sometimes, fear can keep us from taking a good gig. Know when to push through that fear. Even if you struggle with a perceived lack of ability or imposter syndrome, we all find ourselves occasionally having to take a leap of faith and "fake it 'til we make it." Put in the extra work that will keep you from missing opportunities. That's not to say you'll necessarily be ready for every gig that comes your way, but don't let a fearful mindset hold you back.

Say Yes Until You Can Say No - This applies to gigs, recording sessions, rehearsals, networking events, etc. There can be value in all of these things, even if it isn't monetary. Let your ambition drive you in the beginning, and eventually your success will catch up with your aspirations. When to say no will be for you to decide, but until then, don't be afraid to play bars, nursing homes, or even your grandma's birthday party. Start somewhere and eventually you'll find your path.

Always Bring Your "A Game" - Be able to perform to the best of your ability musically and aesthetically each time you pick up your instrument. There are countless stories of musicians being discovered at small or modest venues, so remember that ANY show could potentially change the course of your career. You're playing the long game. Just because you don't see the results of your hard work immediately doesn't mean it won't eventually pay off. Also, you should strive to nail every gig just for the sake of feeling good about your work – it's only going to benefit you in the long run. If you don't practice by taking the little gigs seriously, how do you expect to one day qualify for the big leagues?

Be Versatile - The music world is full of opportunities, and you don't want to be passed over just because you didn't diversify your skills. Even though something isn't currently in your wheelhouse, that doesn't mean you can't pick up a new instrument, learn to sing harmony, or even get the required license to drive the tour bus. One specific example of this would be an acoustic guitar player who can show up and play the banjo or mandolin parts as well.

Skills like this will make you more marketable to potential employers and can be extra income earners. Sometimes a musician may even take a gig that isn't on his or her primary instrument. Two of those musicians include the authors of this book. We've both had to adapt to situations that required us to learn new skills.

Have Reliable Gear - The reality is, the music industry can be competitive, and having great equipment can set you apart from others. At the bare minimum, your gear has to work! You could be the most talented player in the room and if your amp is crackling and popping throughout an entire performance, not only will the other musicians (and the audience) take note, but the person who hired you will as well. People tend to notice the bad more than the good. That being said, we do realize some things are out of your control. But you should do the best you can to help minimize problems. Keep in mind that in most cases, you are responsible for procuring your own equipment. Though the gig might not require a huge investment, you may have to work extra hours at a side job to get the tools you need.

Make New Friends - You'll need people who believe in you, and the more the merrier. Forging new and genuine friendships is crucial to building your network. Also, try to remember names. There are few better ways to build rapport than valuing someone enough to remember who they are. Be authentic and kind. This is the best way to leave a good impression. In the words of the great Maya Angelou, "... people will never forget how you made them feel." So, make them feel good! You never know who might end up recommending you for a gig.

Don't Be Lazy - Laziness can be one of the

biggest contributing factors to failure. To make it in this business, you have to work hard. That concept cannot be reiterated enough. The habits you've developed over the course of your life can be tough to break, but laziness is one worth tackling. Wake up early, make your bed, sip the finest matcha in the world – whatever routine it takes to improve this area of your life, do it. You'll also have to continually monitor your work ethic, as sometimes it can wane over time.

> **THIS BOOK, LIKE ANY OTHER, IS JUST WORDS ON A PAGE; YOU HAVE TO PUT INTENTIONS INTO MOTION.**

Having some success or landing a job with a big artist is not adequate security for your long-term future. Gigs come and go, but life is always there demanding something from us. We're not saying that you have to be a workaholic, but you may have to push yourself a little out of your comfort zone to ensure it will be enough to sustain your career. This book, like any other, is just words on a page; YOU have to put intentions into motion.

Shake the Trees - Go out, network, post flyers, browse Facebook groups, attend jam sessions, and the like. Decent opportunities can even be found online if you look hard enough. While certainly not the end-all-be-all, exploring these avenues can lead to new connections that might help you in the future. Open mic nights, blues jams, and co-writing opportunities abound in many music-centric cities. Try not to write anything off in the beginning.

Take Chances - Whether it's leaving your small

hometown for the big city, buying gear for an audition when you're basically broke, or knocking on doors that may never open, there's always risk involved. But there are countless stories of artists and musicians who initially failed but went on to become wildly successful years later simply because they bet on themselves.

Along the way, you'll run into artists with tons of potential, and who's to say where their careers might go? No one can predict the future. Maybe they'll become the next big thing and you'll be thankful if you get in at the ground level of their career. Remember, every A-level act was an opener at some point in time.

Don't Get Discouraged - For every "yes" you hear, you will hear a hundred "nos." You might audition for ten gigs and land the gig of a lifetime on the eleventh one; remember, you're playing the long game in the music business. Every failure and mistake can become a lesson if you let it, so take it all in stride. Failed auditions, gear issues, dry spells, or having to play a show while you're sick can all be things that will drag you down if you let them.

Keep in mind that a lot of factors go into someone hiring you, and some of those things might be out of your control. There may even be some instances where the people doing the hiring are already leaning toward a certain person for the gig. In that situation, the audition is just a formality and the decision has been made before you even walk through the door. But your relationships are much more important than any blind audition. Keep going. As Jim Carrey once said, "You can fail at what you don't want, so you might as well take a chance on doing what you love."

Not Every Gig is for You - Some bands you'll click

with naturally, some will take work to click with, and others you may never click with at all. You might be right for one gig, but another may be a terrible fit. For example, a band where everyone parties can be absolute hell for someone who doesn't. Where you draw the line between slight compromise and an intolerable environment is up to you. At the end of the day, remember that your contentment and peace hold more value than any gig.

Final Thoughts: No matter your situation, it's good to have an honest inner dialogue to make sure you are conducting your career with all of the above in mind. Again, there's no one-size-fits-all with some of these principles, and your career might look a little different from someone else's. That's okay, just get in where you fit in. Do your best to understand your niche and add new skills as needed. As long as you're working and enjoying what you do, roll with it, baby! Be a chameleon as much as you can, but remember that you will ultimately feel more fulfilled doing something that resonates with you. Also, it's alright if you don't get exactly what you want in the exact way that you want it. New situations will aid you in your journey, so be as open as you can.

ALTHOUGH THE SHOW MIGHT LAST **TWO HOURS,** IT'S THE **OTHER** TWENTY-TWO THAT WILL KEEP YOU **EMPLOYED.**

CHAPTER 2: KEEPING GIGS

So you got a gig. Congrats! Now what? Once you've got a good thing going, you're probably gonna want to keep it! While some jobs will be stepping stones to better opportunities, others might span an entire career. This chapter provides tips for sustaining the gigs that are worth your time and energy.

—

Practice Humility - Being supportive and keeping your ego in check will serve you better than trying to be the smartest guy in the room. As a hired gun, your willingness to learn from others and ability to be a team player are crucial to practicing humility. Don't feel demeaned or get upset just because you're asked to play something differently or perform a task that seems trivial to you. Remember that this is a service industry, and you are never above contributing to the greater good.

Control Your Emotions - At some point, someone is going to have an "off day," and your patience will be tested. You'll be asked to play something in a different way than you want, or maybe an off-handed remark will affect you negatively. In these situations, overreacting could get you in hot water or even fired. Take a second, count to ten, walk away – whatever it takes to calm down. This isn't always easy to do, but giving yourself a minute to process and think through sensitive situations is better than reacting out of anger. Keep in mind the words of James 1:19:

"Everyone should be quick to listen, slow to speak, and slow to become anger."

Be Dependable - Knowing that you can count on someone or something is priceless. Take your car, for example: What if you didn't know from day to day whether or not the brakes would work or the heat would function in the dead of winter? You'd probably trade it in for one you could count on. This is no different from a band or artist keeping you around. Dependability speaks volumes about your character.

Be Nice - Politeness, friendliness, kindness, and empathy are all traits found in successful musicians. Crushing it on stage may feel like your main objective, but consider this: Although the show might last two hours, it's the other twenty-two that will keep you employed. This concept doesn't just apply to the touring world; it's also true when you're in the studio, teaching lessons at a music store, or even playing at a dive bar. Like the old adage goes, you can catch more flies with honey than with vinegar.

Communicate - Always keep an open dialogue with employers, especially when it pertains to job-related issues. If they reach out, respond as soon as you can. Life gets busy, but there's a line between busy and disrespectful. Consider this scenario: An artist needs a band member ASAP and calls three qualified musicians. Two of them don't respond until the following day. One replies almost immediately. Who do you think will get the job? Success in this case is based on the individual's ability to respond in a timely manner, more so than their skills as a player.

Watch Your Words - Many musicians have lost gigs just by opening their mouths when they shouldn't have. You're going to come into contact with people whose views differ vastly from your own, and it's important to be respectful of others. This will help avoid creating a hostile work environment caused by voicing personal opinions. This mentality isn't so much about changing who you are as it is about being mindful of how careless words can impact others. "When in doubt, leave it out." – Carol Costner (Seth's mom)

Appropriateness - There's nothing wrong with chatting it up, cracking jokes, and having fun to keep up morale, but it's important to realize there are subjects and behaviors that aren't appropriate at work. For instance, not everyone is on the same page when it comes to horseplay and roasting, which could get you into hot water. You don't want to be the guy or girl who took things too far, only to get ostracized from the team.

On the subject of conversation, two topics that you should always avoid on gigs are politics and religion. They have the potential to be very emotionally charged and disastrous. From them you can extrapolate other subjects that are best left at home.

Off the Clock - Extracurricular events like birthdays, dinners, and afterparties that involve your co-workers should be respected as environments that could negatively affect your job. Don't take advantage of occasions like these to be inappropriate or overly negative just because you aren't on a tour bus or in a studio. Save gossip and grievances for personal relationships away from your job. Also, be mindful of what you share on social media. You never know who's watching, and anything you post online (drama, hot takes, etc.) could affect your job. The internet is always watching.

Don't Burn Bridges - Remember that repeat business is crucial to longevity in our field, and if you're careless with how you navigate your career, you won't be rehired. Word travels fast, and leaving one gig on a bad note can tarnish your reputation within the whole music community. Keep in mind that in a competitive environment, it's good to go above and beyond to set yourself apart. Although we're all human and we sometimes make mistakes, being continually reckless can ruin your career. So don't burn bridges; strengthen, reinforce, and even clean 'em!

DON'T BURN BRIDGES; STRENGTHEN, REINFORCE, AND EVEN CLEAN 'EM!

Know Your Role - Knowing where you fit into a particular group professionally and personally is paramount. The new guy isn't there to tell the bandleader how to do his job, and the young guy shouldn't take the old guy's seat on the bus – some members have already earned their stripes. Their relationships with one another may have been formed over a long period of time and as much as you want to fit in, try to be conscious of your role in the unspoken hierarchy. We'd all love an immediate level *playing* field (pun intended), but there's no substitute for tenure. In the meantime, just do your job to the best of your ability.

Don't Try TOO Hard - If you're new to a job, don't

try too hard to fit in. Others can see through this and you'll come across as desperate, making those around you uncomfortable. Take a step back and be more of an observer than a participant in the early days. This will allow you to grow into the group more naturally.

Trying too hard to prove your worth may result in overstepping boundaries. For example, a guitar player stepping out in front of the boss for a solo might not be a good look (unless they're explicitly asked to do so). Although they may intend for it to show self-confidence, it can backfire and make the artist feel like the guitarist is trying to outshine them. Self-awareness is key; put your best foot forward, but try not to step on anyone's toes.

Vices and Pitfalls - When it comes to alcohol or any other substance that alters decision making, use moderation. That's a good practice for life in general, but it's especially true when it comes to gigs. First and foremost, we're hired to provide a service, and anything that gets in the way of that will lead to getting fired. Getting ahead in the music industry is hard enough without crossing a line because you had one too many; it's never worth it. Use discretion and be intentional with your actions.

Side note: Don't allow yourself to feel pressure to do something you don't want to do. If you don't want to drink, don't. It's easy to get caught up in the moment, but don't allow yourself to be led to places you don't want to go.

Subbing Gigs - Sometimes you need a substitute, and sometimes you are a substitute. Situations and emergencies happen in life and, as they say, the show must go on. Whether you're the one filling in or the one needing someone to fill in, ensure that you hit a home run and leave the employer pleased. In the case of subbing, do your homework. If you're recommending someone to sub, make sure they're top-notch. This is a good business practice and vital to your reputation. You also never know what connections might be made while subbing and how that might present opportunities down the line.

Studio and Road Etiquette - Knowing how to peacefully coexist on the road or in the studio with your fellow musicians may seem like an obvious and easy thing to do. But you might be surprised at how many people are oblivious to their own behavior. It's not uncommon for someone to get too comfortable and overstep boundaries, so be mindful of how you're impacting others. Are you taking up way too much space with personal items, being inconsiderate with how much noise you're making, or hogging the front lounge aux cable? Etiquette awareness cannot be emphasized enough when it comes to keeping gigs.

Don't Get Too Comfortable - Getting too comfortable can be easy to do, but even if you've been on a gig for many years, remember that (unfortunately) you are replaceable. The good news is, so are gigs! But if you want to keep your gig, don't become stagnant. People notice when someone is just phoning it in. No matter the type of job, whether studio or touring, it's human nature to gradually slip into a routine and become careless (or even think that you can't be let go because of tenure). The reality is that even artists with long-time band members can still decide to go in a different direction. On the flip side, some work environments can become unhealthy and *you* might be the one who needs to go in a different direction. At the end of the day, it's good to remember why you started in the first place and keep the same energy you had in the beginning.

Final Thoughts: So, now that you've read this chapter you'll never have another problem keeping gigs, right? RIGHT?! Well, at least you'll be more well-equipped to handle the slings and arrows of outrageous fortune. Continue to put in the hard work, practice self-awareness and self-control, and stay as mindful of others as you can – kindness and respect will go a long way in helping you keep gigs.

BE IN A **CONSTANT** STATE OF **GROWTH.**

THIS WILL ENSURE

YOUR MUSICAL ABILITIES

KEEP UP WITH THE

DEMANDS

OF A

MODERN

WORKING MUSICIAN.

CHAPTER 3: MUSIC

music

noun. Vocal or instrumental sounds (or both) combined in such a way as to produce beauty of form, harmony, and expression of emotion.

—

So far we've been discussing getting started and securing/maintaining gigs. In this chapter, we'll get into some of the nuts and bolts of making music in a professional capacity. Our aim is to bridge the beginner to the professional by covering a range of topics and keeping you as employable as possible. If any of this is overwhelming or even underwhelming, just keep an open mind and take from it what you can. Music is a beautifully subjective art form and while there are many approaches to it, not all of them are going to lead to a successful career as a hired musician. But real focus and a concerted effort in the following areas will definitely increase your chances of doing just that.

—

First Steps - Before you can make a living performing or recording music, you must first learn how to play. Educating yourself musically is important, whether through a teacher, self instruction, a mentor, or even the prestigious YouTube University. Jam along with your favorite albums and go watch a performance in person. If you're a guitarist, bassist, or even a harmonica player, you may find that tablature is a good place to start as well. All of the aforementioned avenues are great ways to find inspiration for your desired path. Don't *fret* (pun intended) if you didn't start your journey early – it's never too late. Be in a constant state of growth. This will ensure your musical abilities keep up with the demands of a modern working musician.

Playing by Ear - Being able to identify what you're hearing and knowing how to react, recreate, and perform it is essential when communicating musically; and the quicker the better! This will help you learn and memorize songs, jam with other musicians, and speed up the process of having to cram for that last-minute gig. Once refined, your ear is like your musical "gut instinct," and it will rarely steer you wrong. The good news is that this ability can be improved over time and compounds itself.

Improvising - The ability to create music spontaneously in the moment will serve you well. This is especially relevant in genres such as jazz, where improvisation is a huge part of the experience. If this is new to you, don't be afraid to start simple or make mistakes. You won't sound like John Coltrane in the beginning; achieving mastery is a long process. Come up with your own riffs, jam with a buddy, and play along with tracks online. Improvising for fun should coincide with learning the building blocks of music like scales, chords, arpeggios, and rhythms. When you balance the fun and educational aspects, this will coalesce into a well-rounded skill set as an improviser.

Understanding Music Theory - You don't have to have a doctorate if that's not what your musical interests call for, but a general knowledge of how music works is important. Knowing key signatures, time signatures, and Roman numeral analysis; understanding how basic harmony functions; and having the ability to transpose on the fly are just some of the skills you will need for certain jobs. For example, if you're accompanying a vocalist and they need to change keys, it's invaluable to be able to roll with it and play in the new key. A great book on music theory is Tonal Harmony (*Kostka, Payne, Almén*); it's widely used by colleges and private instructors. While not essential for every type of gig, a solid foundation in music theory will open up possibilities and new doors that might otherwise be locked.

Reading - Here's another area in which you don't have to be Dr. "So-And-So" to get a gig, but knowing how to read music will definitely keep you from missing opportunities. This can encompass sight reading, chart reading, the Nashville number system, or other forms of written music. Which form you use will vary from gig to gig and genre to genre. No matter the type of music you're reading, becoming proficient at it will take time and effort. Hire an instructor or even find some music online to work on. From the orchestra to the cover band, knowing how to read is essential to maximizing your potential.

Practicing - A common thread among working musicians is their willingness to continue practicing. While this is somewhat of a personal experience and results may vary, at a certain point we all have to put in some work. Even twenty minutes of focused practice a day can make a huge difference; we hope it's encouraging news that a little can go a long way and you don't have to practice eight hours a day to see results. Consistently using a metronome or click, working on ear training and theory, improving dexterity, and especially playing along to your favorite albums can all be great ways to level up. As a hired musician, you can anticipate a challenging gig at some point, and you'll be glad that you have good practice habits in place. Following that thought, where and when you do your homework is also important. If you've had the material for weeks and are running through the set right before you go on stage, you've waited too late and may need to re-evaluate your practice habits.

FROM THE ORCHESTRA TO THE COVER BAND, KNOWING HOW TO READ IS ESSENTIAL TO MAXIMIZING YOUR POTENTIAL.

Serve the Song - Knowing what (and when) to play is a huge part of your job as a hired musician. This is a valuable skill that may take a while to develop, but it's essential in the service-based sector of music. In an effort to serve the song, self-awareness is important. There's nothing wrong with being confident, but don't let that bleed over into cockiness. Always be open to feedback. Unless you're expressly hired for your distinct sound or asked for your input from the producer or artist, it's better to be a blank canvas. Also, it's important to be genre appropriate no matter what you are playing – in other words, shredding a guitar solo over Brown Eyed Girl might not get you the callback. If it's a "play the part from the album" gig, then stick to the script. But for a jam band or improvisation-based group, there will be more room for interpretation. In both instances, you should play what is right for the music. If you're unsure of what to play, use this quick priority list of questions (in order of importance):

    1. What does the boss/artist want?

2. What does the bandleader want?
3. What's on the recording?
4. What do YOU want?

This can be somewhat of a flexible list, but it's not a bad place to start. If you're unsure, most bandleaders won't (and shouldn't) mind pertinent questions in an effort to nail the job. Obviously, if it's your band then you make the rules, but if not, these are some great principles.

Performance - Performance is where the rubber meets the road. When the time comes, can you pull off in front of a live audience what you practiced at home? Whether during a concert or a studio session, accurately executing the music while dealing with factors such as nerves, stress, late nights/early mornings, and other curveballs can be a skill that takes time to acquire. One way this skill can be developed is by taking every gig seriously – even the coffee shop show where no one is listening. These performances will serve as a training ground for that bucket list venue down the road and shouldn't be taken lightly.

Studio Chops - Versatility and execution are the name of the game regarding studio work. Being able to adapt to different genres as a player, nail the part, and have a wide range of gear at your disposal is crucial. Your proficiency on a single instrument will need to be at a considerably high level. On another *note* (here we go again), some musicians even get into producing, mixing, and mastering projects themselves. Casting a wide net can give you the best chance of staying busy.

Execution - We've already touched on practicing, but one of the main ingredients to executing a flawless performance lies in HOW you practice. There are many things you can do in the practice room that will help you when you're on the spot. Some of these can include: practicing a part until it's a part of you, filming yourself or practicing in front of the mirror, playing while standing as opposed to sitting, or even performing in front of a couple of friends and your dog Herbie to get the jitters out. At the end of the day, a hired musician's ability to perform under pressure will separate the wheat from the chaff.

Final Thoughts: Being a musician is not a typical 9-to-5 job (and that job is never really done). You can always find something to work on, and there's absolutely no substitute for putting in the time. Where to focus your energy will be up to you. It's always good to lean into your strengths, but be sure you're also devoting time to areas that may need work. Consulting a trusted mentor or teacher may help you identify some blind spots. These could be sight reading, ear training, showmanship, technique, or a number of other things. Whatever these issues are, take the necessary steps to be the best YOU that you can be. Keep in mind that comparison is the thief of joy, and your next steps may look different from someone else's. Most of us have big dreams of being on a big stage, but unless we've put in the practice time, it will be a much harder road – and much less fun.

MAYBE TODAY YOU'RE **SPLITTING** A BIG MAC WITH YOUR **ROOMMATE,** BUT EVENTUALLY YOU'LL BE ABLE TO MAKE IT A **COMBO MEAL.**

CHAPTER 4: MONEY

money

noun. Any item or medium of exchange that is accepted by people for the payment of goods and services.

As we stated in Chapter 3, being a musician isn't a typical 9-to-5 job, so it's safe to assume that the financial aspects are anything but typical as well. You literally and figuratively can't *afford* to be complacent regarding your finances. In an industry that tends to ebb and flow, it would be a crime not to dedicate an entire chapter to navigating the financial aspects of this field. We'll cover subjects like how to make, save, and spend money; pay negotiation; debt; and some practical tips.

Getting into hard numbers would be challenging here, as there are several factors that go into how much each gig pays. Union scales, varying budgets (based on each unique gig), negotiation, and other details make getting into specifics difficult. That being said, there's still plenty of information about finances in this chapter, and we've also included a resource list at the end of this book.

Making Money - There are a lot of ways to bring in money as a musician: live performances, in-studio and remote recording, livestream events, merchandise, digital music services, teaching – the list goes on and on. In this section, we'll touch on a few common ways musicians go about making money.

Live Performances

Live performances can take place in some of the following settings:
- Park or street busking.
- Bars and clubs.
- Weddings, bar mitzvahs, and other private events.
- Churches.
- Cruise ships.
- Theaters.
- Arenas and stadiums.

While it's not an exhaustive list, this should give you an idea of what types of environments exist in the live performance realm. Venues vary depending on the gig, but there is money to be made no matter what your goals are.

Depending on the business model (or lack thereof), how you're categorized in terms of employment will vary. Independent contracting, temporary or sub work, salaried employee, or even just a handshake agreement are a few of the ways you can be compensated. How often you're paid is up to each company or employer and is typically on an hourly, daily, weekly, bi-weekly, monthly, or per-show basis.

Studio Work

Studio work can take place in some of the following settings:
- Commercial recording studio.
- Small project studio.

- Home studio.
- Mobile and portable studios.

    Whether you're recording from home on a laptop or at Abbey Road, being a studio musician can be a good way to pay the bills. Depending on the situation, you may even find more fulfillment in this type of work as opposed to live performances. You'll also play a more integral role in the creative process behind the recording.

    Typically you'll be paid union scale, hourly, day-to-day, per album, or on a song-by-song basis. Union scale refers to the minimum wage scales used by the American Federation of Musicians to pay musicians on recording dates. There are also other ways to be compensated for playing on recordings, including points and other forms of residuals. Points (AKA "percentage" or "producer" points) are a percentage of revenues earned on the song(s) or album. Residuals are payments received when a work is reused in a different medium.

    We'll delve deeper into the subject of road dogs vs. studio cats later in the book. To be content-conscious, we've left the details out of this chapter for fear of *barking* up the wrong tree (you guessed it ... pun intended).

Teaching

    There will always be a need for music teachers and tutors, which is good news for the working musician. Private lessons from home, virtual teaching, collegiate education, private music schools, workshops, masterclasses, and even posting video content on a website can all be ways to support yourself financially. There are several schools of thought on how to teach music, but the good news is you don't have to have a degree from a prestigious college to teach. It certainly doesn't hurt, but it isn't necessarily a requirement. While everyone's experience as a musician will differ, the foundational principles of music remain the same. Fortunately, there is a plethora of teaching material already available to pull from. Publishing companies like Mel Bay, Hal Leonard, and even online resources like YouTube are great ways to get started. Or, you could even craft your own curriculum entirely.

The prospect of teaching can seem a bit intimidating if you're new to it, but as with anything else, you will learn as you go. Determine what level of student you're best suited to instruct (beginner, intermediate, advanced) and do some research to find a competitive rate that works for your local scene. Once you've found your niche, you're ready to roll. Many people make a good living teaching, and one of the most rewarding aspects of the job is knowing that you're setting up a new generation of musicians for success.

Intellectual Property

Writing and publishing songs, creating and selling merch, authoring a book about the music business (cha-ching!) – these are just a few ways you can capitalize on your original ideas. The advantages can range from creative control and fulfillment to increased earning potential. If your goal is to play as an instrumentalist covering other people's parts, then understand that isn't YOUR intellectual property you're working with. So bear in mind that to maximize profit, you may want to ask yourself how you can monetize what you're creating.

Saving Money - Saving money is easier said than done, but it's essential to longevity as a career musician.

You may have seasons where income you earned previously will get you by, and you'll be thankful for the funds you've set aside. That money will act as a buffer to help bridge the gaps between gigs. Life is unpredictable, and putting money back can help mitigate damage when something unexpected happens. And you can be sure something's gonna happen (misplaced, broken, or stolen gear; car trouble; Herbie's vet bill; etc.). In addition to getting you through the tough times, saving money can also decrease stress, which will allow for more level-headed decision making.

There are many approaches to saving (as well as books and courses on the subject), but the basic principle is that once you've begun to actually make money, you should take the next step and live on less than you make. From there, the natural progression is to evolve beyond the paycheck to paycheck existence into saving. Saving money is simple in principle, but it does require a lot of focus and discipline. Your overall mindset of how you live your daily life has to change, especially if you've never been one to really pay attention to your money habits. Take an honest look at how much you make vs. how much you spend to see if your decisions are sound.

The next step is to start investing when you find yourself in a position to do so. Obviously, don't get ahead of yourself, but when the time comes, find a way to make your money work for you. Many musicians are paid on a per-gig basis, and investing can be a great way to generate income beyond this limitation. This can include options like IRAs, money market accounts, the stock market, day trading, or the housing market. Maybe today you're splitting a Big Mac with your roommate, but eventually you'll be able to make it a combo meal. Ha!

Spending Money – There are a lot of ways to spend your money; some are wise, some are not. Some expenses are necessary to execute your job, while others are more frivolous. Just because you don't have the latest gear, expensive show clothes, or the flashiest software doesn't mean you can't do your job. Don't totally ignore these aspects – just be sure to evaluate the necessity of your spending. Touring, in particular, can make you forget your financial responsibilities back home. It can feel like a vacation, especially in the beginning, and there are countless ways to spend your money out on the road.

After the basics are covered (meals, utilities, housing, transportation, insurance, etc.), we enter the unique realm of what is required of the modern musician. One of the most expensive aspects of this will most likely be your gear. While each situation is unique, making sure you have the right equipment and that it's well-maintained is crucial no matter the gig. Sometimes you have to spend money to make money, and if you can't actually make music with your current rig, you can't do your job. For example, smacking your keyboard to get it to work may mean it's time to upgrade!

Other worthy investments can include taking lessons, driving to jam sessions, attending a concert, buying coffee for a fellow musician, or even taking a seasoned pro to lunch in exchange for advice. These are all great ways to invest in your future and strengthen your network. Building and maintaining relationships with fellow industry people can be one of the strongest ingredients for success. The folks who believe in you will recommend you for future gigs, so take advantage of every rapport-building opportunity you can, even if it means spending money.

Rates and Negotiating - Discussions about compensation can sometimes be daunting and uncomfortable.

But negotiating a starting rate or talking to your current employer about a pay increase can be necessary for financial survival. Remember that ultimately, no one will care about your business like you will, so the responsibility is yours. Advocating for healthy work environments and fair pay will fall on you – don't be afraid to pursue an amount that makes you comfortable.

NEGOTIATING A STARTING RATE OR TALKING TO YOUR CURRENT EMPLOYER ABOUT A PAY INCREASE CAN BE NECESSARY FOR FINANCIAL SURVIVAL.

Depending on the area in which you're operating, you'll either set your own rate or come to an agreement with a second party. The point of contact regarding money on the touring side of things will most likely be the manager, business manager, tour manager, and/or bandleader. But the artist will probably have final say in these matters. Use tact, intentionality, self-awareness, and kindness when approaching this sensitive subject. Also, keep in mind that if you're looking a good situation in the face, you'll probably just want to say yes. Not every job calls for negotiating.

Debt - Being a career musician has its difficulties, and one way to make it even harder on yourself is to have a pile of debt and bill collectors knocking at your door. Expenses like credit card debt, car payments, and secondary education costs are all hindrances to your peace of mind as a musician. Those dreams of playing on a hit record or performing at Wembley Stadium may be more difficult to realize when you're drowning in 20% Petco (where the pets go) financing charges.

Practical Tips

1. Limit non-essential purchases. That's not to say don't enjoy yourself from time to time; just be mindful of expenses and have the discipline to avoid unnecessary costs when you can. Remember, you can spend today, but rent's due tomorrow.

2. Pack a meal for long commutes, as dining out can really add up. Sandwiches and homemade beef jerky can be so much cheaper than a gas station bender.

3. Keep track of your purchases and file them under your expenses at the end of the year. This will depend on your status (W-2, 1099, etc.), and you'll want to consult a tax professional to see what best fits your situation.

4. Get insurance for all your musical equipment. Instruments, cases, in-ear monitors, and even your computer can fall into this category.

5. Have some cash on hand. This is good for emergency situations and can keep you from overspending.

6. Take advantage of free online resources. This semester, take that YouTube course on saving you've had bookmarked.

7. Talk to – and learn from – people who are good with money. Run large purchases that you're unsure about by a trusted friend or mentor. They can help you stay grounded in reality and necessity.

Hired Musician

Final Thoughts: The music industry (and life, actually) is ever-changing, and success is not always linear. Our goal with this chapter was to present an overview of some of the music industry's many financial facets to aid in that success. Obviously we couldn't explore everything in one chapter, but we wanted to at least touch on some basics. Bear in mind, there may be times when a side hustle or two is necessary to get by. You might even have to work a less-than-desirable job for a while. But don't let that discourage you from staying the course with the hope of eventually doing what you love for a living.

REMEMBER, YOUR **SUCCESS** IS BASED ON **MORE** THAN JUST HOW **WELL** YOU PLAY; IT ALSO HINGES ON HOW WELL YOU PLAY **WITH OTHERS.**

CHAPTER 5: MINDSET

mindset

noun. The established set of attitudes held by someone.

—

    The crux of this book is how to survive in the music industry, and of particular importance is the psychology behind that pursuit. Your overall attitude, being a team player, hustling, and thinking positively all fall under this umbrella and are included in this chapter. It's imperative to keep the right mindset because your outlook on life can be just as important as your circumstances (if not more so). The music industry can be volatile, ever-changing, and unpredictable, making it a breeding ground for negative thoughts. Not every day will be sunshine and roses, but keeping a positive, driven, and open-minded approach can help you navigate the mental stress that comes with the territory.

—

    Overall Attitude - Every career has its challenges, and jobs within the music biz are no exception. A positive attitude will help every area of your life, and this is especially true when times get tough at work. Remember that you're in the people business, and your demeanor and actions will affect those around you. This could mean keeping a smile on your face even when you're not feeling it, or at least doing your best to leave your problems at the door. *Insert "fake it 'til you make it" platitude here.* Having a good overall attitude will also positively impact your personal goals like health and finances, or even friendships and relationships. This may not feel like it directly applies to your music career, but in a way *you* are the business, and your daily attitude and actions will overlap from the personal to the professional.

You Are the Business - You yourself are the brick and mortar: human resources (1099s, sub-contracting), accounts receivable (reminding clients to remit payment), market research and strategies (networking, gear), and even the janitor (get a haircut and clean that guitar). In a conventional job, you may have easy access to these things within a company, but as a musician, you take on a lot of these roles personally. Early on, the gigs might not be as lucrative as they eventually will be. Obviously the goal here is to make a living doing what you love, but when you're starting out, you can think of it like an internship. We all have to pay our dues to get to that next level. An example of this can include playing on your first session or gig pro bono or at a reduced rate to give the client an idea of how well you play.

Be a Team Player - This concept applies interpersonally as well as musically. You wouldn't (or shouldn't) talk over someone who is telling a story, so by the same token, you should not play over someone in a band setting when it's your turn to take a backseat. Sometimes less is more, and the space between the notes is as important as the notes themselves.

Be social with your co-workers. We're not saying you have to conform to the group every time, but it doesn't hurt to build comradery with your bandmates over a bucket of popcorn and that new Spider-Man flick. Different gigs will have different demands, and you're responsible for more than just playing your instrument. Covering the basics (being punctual, knowing your material, treating people well) is probably a given, but you should also go above and beyond. Remind those around you that you're happy to be there and eager to help. All of this is said assuming you're being treated well and compensated fairly. Remember, your success is based on more than just how well you play – it also hinges on how well you play with others.

Hustling - Just because there's food on the table now doesn't mean next month's groceries are free. This means that unless you're wealthy and insulated from the need to work, you've got to keep cash coming in. Multiple streams of income are the lifeblood of the modern musician. You can keep your side hustles under the umbrella of music (teaching, music production, live sound, etc.), but there's also no shame in diversifying and getting involved outside of the industry. Many musicians have side jobs in fields like real estate, food service, rideshare (Uber, Lyft), remote work, or even writing a book about getting and keeping gigs. Don't feel like you've failed by pursuing other avenues. It's a must for every musician, and a good idea for most people, to expand their forms of income.

Thinking Positively - We almost left this one out because of how implicit and similar to "Overall Attitude" it can be, but a positive outlook on life is your ticket to happiness, and we couldn't justify omitting it. Approach everything you do with the idea that it's leading you to the goals you've always dreamed about. Obviously not every single thing you attempt will be successful; that's just life. Failed auditions and missed opportunities are all part of the journey. But if you get into the habit of assuming the worst, or predicting a failure before you even try, you will set yourself up for disappointment for no reason. In fact, this paragraph could have been titled "Avoiding Negativity," because negativity will eat you alive if you let it.

Clocking In - In a way, the job starts as soon as you agree to a gig. The commute to the venue or studio, making sure you have the right tools for the gig, preparing charts, and listening to the songs are all examples of the work that happens once you say yes. There are certainly hurry up and wait moments, when the playing portion of your day pales in comparison to the time spent waiting around. Some musicians assume the job starts when the music begins and don't realize they're on the clock even when they don't have an instrument in their hands. But you can view traveling in a tour bus, flying on a plane, or even socializing at a bar with bandmates as being on the clock.

Avoiding Drama - It's important to stay out of the trenches of interpersonal conflict on the job. Sometimes the lines between friend and co-worker can get blurry and lead to misunderstandings, so be aware of this risk. Tour buses and recording studios are our workplaces and at the end of the day, we're there to do a job. As you become more comfortable on a job, you may have to remind yourself to temper your tongue. Remember, you can't take back words once they've been spoken, and the old saying, "If you ain't got nothing nice to say, don't say anything at all" is a valuable phrase.

The Golden Rule - Treat others as you want to be treated. This applies to everyone from top to bottom. It's common sense to treat your boss well, but you will most likely find yourself spending much more time interacting with other people. Obviously it's just the right thing to do, but treating people right can also make you stand out – and standing out will lead to more work in the sometimes self-serving atmosphere of the music business. Your words and actions have ripple effects, so make sure you are treating people with the same respect you want for yourself.

Morals and Ethics - Don't compromise your ethos just to further your career. If your gut tells you that you're making concessions to fit into an environment that doesn't align with your morals, it's better to just walk away. No gig is worth losing your integrity. There will be other, better opportunities available to you down the road.

YOUR MINDSET CAN DETERMINE YOUR OUTLOOK, WHICH CAN SHAPE YOUR ACTIONS, AND YOUR ACTIONS WILL BRING YOU CLOSER TO YOUR DESIRED OUTCOME.

Humility - No matter who you are or what you have accomplished, there's always something new to learn. Some of the greatest musicians are known to be the most humble. This isn't a coincidence. Humility leads to an open mind when it comes to learning and progressing. If you get to the point where you believe you know it all, not only will you stop growing, but you may also rub people the wrong way. Being humble will make you more approachable and relatable and can lead to people recommending you for work. Arrogance, on the other hand, will push people away.

Determination - It's a well-known fact that making a living in the music industry is difficult. Challenges and setbacks will arise no matter who you are. Determination and grit are going to carry you through the tough times, take you to the better times, and help you land that one big opportunity that can change the entire trajectory of your career. Maybe you've auditioned for ten bands and have failed at every single one. Who's to say the eleventh audition isn't the one that will be life-changing? There are countless real-world examples of people finding success after sticking it out for many, many years: Bill Withers, Leonard Cohen, Sheryl Crow, Andrea Bocelli, Willie Nelson, Bonnie Raitt, Sia, Thelonius Monk ... the list goes on and on. Staying determined is a requirement in a career full of the word "no," and remember, all it takes is one "yes" to change everything. Have courage in the face of adversity – you could be on the cusp of your magnum opus.

Entitlement - To put it bluntly, the world owes you nothing, let alone a cushy gig that's exactly what you've always dreamed about. Of course we all want to achieve our goals and dreams, but thinking and acting like we deserve them is dangerous territory. Peers and employers will pick up on this mindset, and you might miss out on work because of it. Never feel or act like something is "beneath" you; doing so will give everyone around you a bad impression and bring the overall vibe down.

Adaptability - As a musician, you will inevitably face inconsistencies – pay scales, types of gigs, personalities, styles of music, and more. Different situations will require different versions of you, and the ability to roll with the punches will help keep your rent paid. You'll also have periods where doing something less than ideal might be necessary. Maybe it's playing a genre of music that isn't your favorite, or teaching music when that isn't your forte.

Whatever the case, be prepared to suck it up and focus on the end game (whatever yours may be). Finding a balance between doing what you need to do and doing what you want to do is an ongoing process. Adapting to each new circumstance (favorable or unfavorable) will help you build character and enable you to face any career challenge that comes your way.

Confidence - Out in the real world, you've got to believe in yourself before anyone else will believe in you. Not only will you encounter people who are unsupportive, some of them may even try to tear you down, and having confidence can carry you through those negative experiences. Playing guitar alone all day in your bedroom is fun, but if your desire is to build a career, at some point you need to show the world what you've got. This obviously takes a lot of confidence. It may come more naturally for some people than for others, but it is something you can work at improving. The more you do something, the easier it will become. It's rare to find someone who isn't at least a little self-conscious when performing on stage for the first time or letting someone hear their first composition. But with time, confidence can be built. So, how can we build confidence? Repetitive practice, practicing in front of a mirror, analyzing recordings of yourself, seeking constructive feedback, setting achievable goals, and engaging in positive self-talk are some surefire ways to do this.

Blind Ambition - Considering all the struggles in the music business, sometimes a little naivety or healthy delusion can complement persistence. If someone in the beginning of their career fully understood the hardships that come with this industry, they might give up too soon and never realize their dreams. That's not to say you should bury your head in the sand, as there's nothing wrong with thinking ahead – just don't let fear dictate your every step.

Desperation - Desperation can cloud your judgment and make others hesitant to work with you. If you feel like your back is against the wall, you may be more inclined to make impulsive decisions. Try to take a step back when things aren't going as well as you want them to, and understand that this too shall pass. Don't make a decision when you're desperate; wait until the dust settles, and what's meant for you will find a way to you. People are not stupid, and they usually know that a desperate person may resort to using manipulation to get what they want. This can make people uncomfortable, especially from the vantage point of an employer. It can also be annoying to be hounded for a gig, or a response to an email or text message. Just be as calm, cool, and collected as you can, even if it feels like the light at the end of the tunnel is dim.

Handling Stress - There are many healthy ways for people to combat stress: exercise, meditation, a peaceful walk, or even defeating Bowser as an Italian plumber. Don't hesitate to embrace whatever helps you unwind or relax. There are also unhealthy ways to cope with stress as well, and they have been known to derail many careers. Substance abuse and other reckless behaviors are not a healthy response to stress. They can ostracize you from the music community and even ruin a life.

Motivation and Inspiration - The music business can wear down even the strongest of people, and sometimes it's easy to forget why you started working in the industry in the first place. When you're pursuing a passion instead of chasing a paycheck, you have to stay driven and keep the fires stoked, or else you may become disillusioned and quit. At that point, you could've just pursued a six-figure corporate job with benefits and health insurance. There's absolutely nothing wrong with that, but even if you're just wanting to play music as a hobby, you still have to stay motivated and inspired to progress. If you're looking for ways to do this, try listening to or playing along with new music, go see a great live band, study new music concepts by taking a course or lessons, or just find time to sit down and play for the fun of it.

Final Thoughts: The goal of this chapter was to highlight the importance of your mindset. Your mindset can determine your outlook, which can shape your actions, and your actions will bring you closer to your desired outcome. If you're reading this book, then that desired outcome is probably getting and keeping gigs. So be confident but not egotistical, keep a positive attitude, and be a team player. These mindsets will make you indispensable to employers.

TALES OF OVERNIGHT SUCCESS MAKE FOR DECENT STORYTELLING, BUT THEY NEVER PAINT THE FULL PICTURE.

CHAPTER 6: MYTHS

myth

noun. A widely held but false belief or idea.

People have a tendency to either glamorize or demonize the music industry and its lifestyle. From the outside looking in, it's easy to let your imagination run wild. Thoughts of being rich and famous or penniless and addicted cast a shadow over what most working musicians know to be true. One side seems out of reach, and the other is obviously tragic. Believe it or not, there's an entire middle class of professionals who make a solid living and have a healthy home life. We're not trying to deny the challenges that come with this career (hard work, late nights, sacrifices, etc.), or even the temptation of unhealthy behaviors, but our hope is that after reading this chapter you will walk away with a better understanding of this commonly misunderstood field.

Myth:
I'm going to be rich and famous!

Truth:
This is certainly a reality for some people and we're definitely rooting for you, but this industry can be full of ups and downs. You might be on top of the world one day and

looking for a new gig the next. It may sound cliche, but you HAVE to do it for the love of music and with the knowledge that it will require some hard work. Fame and fortune can be fleeting, and that road to your mansion on Rodeo Drive can be long and winding.

Myth:
I'm going to end up penniless and addicted!

Truth:
While there are countless cautionary tales of wasted opportunity and potential, it's a myth to believe that this is inevitable. Everyone can avoid being a statistic. It can certainly take some self-discipline to stay away from bad habits, but it's very doable and absolutely worth the effort. Having family or friends who hold you accountable, keeping a close eye on your spending, and learning how to say no to damaging decisions can help you sustain a long and healthy career.

Myth:
If you do what you love, you'll never work a day in your life.

Truth:
Of course we all understand the intention behind this saying, but even in music, "work" can be a four-letter word. Burnout, fatigue, and frustration aren't absent from the field of music. However, the joy of pursuing your passion and doing what you want can make it more of a labor of love. "If you do what you love, you'll never HAVE to work a day in your life" might be a more accurate sentiment.

Myth:
Being a musician is one big party.

Truth:
There's sometimes a stigma or perception from people outside of the music business that being a musician is one big party. Musicians can be thought of or portrayed as lazy, and the industry as nothing more than sex, drugs, and rock 'n' roll. That's not to say that music can't take you to some interesting places with interesting circumstances and interesting people, but it's not realistic or even sustainable to think that the party never ends and that no work is required. There are plenty of musicians taking care of themselves physically and working hard to achieve their goals.

Myth:
Success will happen quickly.

Truth:
Tales of overnight success make for decent storytelling, but they never paint the full picture. Hard work and persistence over time usually precede anything worth having – and anything worth having can only truly be appreciated through working hard to acquire it. Even if success did come overnight, it's likely that the recipient wouldn't have the capacity to handle it with care. It would be very easy for them to take it for granted and quite possibly squander their success. This mentality can also cause someone to quit when things get tough – and rest assured, they likely will get tough at some point in your career.

Myth:
Music is not a "real job."

Truth:
This tired trope is only ever used by those outside of the music industry. The people actually working inside of it

know better. Albeit less common and a "labor of love," as described a couple of paragraphs back, music can absolutely be as legitimate, rewarding, and taxing as any other field. As of May 2022, according to the U.S. Bureau of Labor Statistics, there are around 173,000 jobs for musicians and singers, with a median pay of $39.14 per hour. The overall median pay for all occupations in the U.S. was about $22 per hour during this same time period. The industry definitely has its troubles, but just because your Great Aunt Karen can't conceptualize what a career in music looks like doesn't mean that it isn't a (very) "real job."

Myth:
Talent is always rewarded.

Truth:
We hate to break it to you, but that Spanish Phrygian scale you've mastered doesn't matter as much as your manners. Just because you're the best musician in the room doesn't mean you'll have the best gig in the room. In fact, it doesn't even guarantee that you will have a gig at all – there's just more to it than that. Your personality, ability to follow directions, and amiability are huge in this field. Make sure to keep your interpersonal muscles as in-shape as your musical muscles. What a shame it would be to have the skills of a Jaco, Tedesco, or Chambers and never be able to share those skills with others because you can't get along with people and hold down a job.

Myth:
Talent always outweighs hard work.

Truth:
Most musicians know they have to work hard. Even if

someone is gifted with natural ability, mastery isn't effortless, and each gig can have unique demands. Some people may have to work harder than others, but the goal is the same regardless of the path to it. If a talented player puts in zero effort and does a terrible job, they won't get called back. Conversely, a lesser musician putting in a ton of effort might nail that same gig, increasing the likelihood of future work. Which musician would YOU rather hire? (Obviously the one who delivers.)

So don't be the talented person who bums everyone out by not working hard! Talent can be a crutch for some people. When something comes easy to us, the tendency can be to take it for granted and coast if we aren't careful. Don't just phone it in, or you may find yourself falling through the cracks of the industry.

Myth:
This gig is a waste of my time.

Truth:
Almost every gig has SOME value. Even if it ends up being a nightmare, you'll at least walk away knowing what kind of jobs you don't want to do. We've all had to learn this lesson, sometimes several times over. At the bare minimum, try to look for the good in every situation and if you agree to a gig, give it 100%. You may even meet someone who helps you out later on in your career, and you'll be glad they heard you at your best. Treat every gig equally and remember that you're helping your future self learn skills for when you DO get that big opportunity.

Eventually yes, there will be gigs that aren't the best use of your time, but keep an open mind in the beginning, because you never know what could come out of them.

Myth:
It's NEVER my fault when I don't get the gig.

Truth:
Admitting that you've failed or done something wrong is never fun. But being unable to admit when you are the problem can prevent you from succeeding as a hired musician. Some people operate under delusion, while others may even border on narcissism. The reality is, sometimes our actions (or lack thereof) do keep us from getting a gig. You should always be open to exploring reasons why the desired outcome did not happen. Develop a fierce sense of self-awareness and chat with a trusted friend or counselor for input if you're wondering why things aren't working out. These actions will help you course-correct if there's an issue and increase your chances of landing jobs in the future.

Myth:
It's ALWAYS my fault when I don't get the gig.

Truth:
If you blame yourself for every gig or audition that doesn't go your way, it's likely that your self-perception is skewed. Failure is not always a reflection of your talent or dedication. There are usually more elements at play, such as budget restraints, nepotism, or chemistry. The variables are endless. Like we talked about in Chapter 1, many factors go into the hiring process. Some of those factors are within your control, and some are not. Focus on the ones that are. Hone your craft, network, treat everyone with kindness, acquire the right tools, and even buy some leather pants if the gig calls for it. All kidding aside, it's not always your fault when you don't get a gig.

Myth:
I'm making good money ... Now I can relax.

Truth:
By now you're probably tired of us saying that the music business is unpredictable and in a constant state of flux. We'll risk the redundancy to ensure that you don't become complacent when the money is rolling in. Life can always throw you a curveball, and things happen like tour cancellations, medical emergencies, natural disasters, your main employer taking extended time off or retiring, or you being let go. You've got to plan ahead so that these circumstances won't overwhelm you if and when they happen. Invest your money, teach, gig between tours and sessions, learn a new trade, or even find outside sources of income available to you – whether that be music-adjacent or something completely unrelated. Just be mindful of the fact that your income is subject to change.

IT DOESN'T MATTER IF YOU'VE WORKED TIRELESSLY FOR YEARS OR EVEN KNOW SOMEONE WHO KNOWS SOMEONE; A SENSE OF ENTITLEMENT WILL NOT GET YOU FAR.

Myth:
I DESERVE a good gig.

Truth:
No, you don't. It doesn't matter if you've worked tirelessly for years or even know someone who knows someone; a sense of entitlement will not get you far in this business. Others will pick up on cues like your tone, body language, and behavior patterns, signaling to them that something is socially off. This is going to hurt your chances of getting

gigs and is a toxic mindset. Instead of asking yourself what you deserve, try to reframe your thinking to a posture of openness and gratefulness for every opportunity that comes your way.

Myth:
My self-worth is defined by my gig.

Truth:
It's obviously very important to make a living, but your career doesn't speak to your inherent value as a person. Don't wrap up too much of your identity in your job. Your humanity defines who you are long before that does, and basing your self-worth on what you do can lead to unfulfillment and even depression. Friendships, relationships, hobbies, and health are just some of the things that eclipse work, so make sure you're categorizing them appropriately.

Myth:
Having a big gig will make me happy.

Truth:
Sorry to burst your proverbial bubble, but thousands of screaming fans, millions of dollars in the bank, and adoration from your peers won't (ultimately) lead to lasting happiness. That's not to diminish the excitement and satisfaction of having a killer job, but it's more to highlight the importance of maintaining a work/life balance. The two can work in tandem, but don't expect happiness to hang solely upon bragging rights because you have a big gig (something that's, at least in part, out of your control).

Myth:
Touring is a dream come true.

Truth:
While touring can definitely be fun and enjoyable, it can also be taxing. There's no one-size-fits-all regarding road gigs; some people love them, some hate them. Most of us are somewhere between these two extremes. Bear in mind, the circumstances of a road gig are going to influence your level of enjoyment. A small van full of farts and Doritos en route to your cousin's friend's floor to sleep isn't going to be as fun as a tour bus ride to a nice hotel. The gap between real and ideal can be wide, even when you're traveling to or through beautiful places. The perks are obvious, but there will be times when you'll have to just roll with the changes and make the most of the cons of touring.

Myth:
They hired ME, so I can play however I want.

Truth:
If that's how the person hiring you sees it, then great! Yes, you absolutely can. But it's worth considering that if you decide to go rogue and overplay, you may accidentally find yourself out of a job. If you're unsure of what the boss or bandleader wants, ask. No one has telepathy, and it's better to be safe than sorry. If you just decide to play however you want, your employers could potentially be put off or even pissed off. Set your ego aside and accommodate the gig.

Myth:
The only thing a musician has to worry about is playing their instrument.

Truth:
This is one we all wish were true. How great would it be if

our fridges stayed full while we just sipped coffee and solely focused on the instrument we play? Unfortunately, that's just not the reality of the situation. So, what else *do* you have to worry about doing? Networking, being on time, wearing the proper attire, and anything else from Chapter 1 of this book are some of those things. So many other things outside of actually playing our instruments are required of us. It would be wise to give them all some thought and attention.

Final Thoughts: Separating fact from fiction is no small task and is best aided by personal experience. Experience is a word we've used a lot in this book, and for good reason: It will help cut through the noise and become your inner compass on the journey to a successful music career. We've included as many important myths as we could in this chapter, but no doubt there are more for you to dispel. Remember, truth is an ally on your quest, so stay away from myths propagated by those outside of the industry.

FOCUS ON YOUR GOALS AND HOW TO **ATTAIN THEM,** KEEPING IN MIND THAT NO ONE CAN **PREDICT** THE FUTURE AND YOU CAN'T **TURN BACK TIME** TO CHANGE THE PAST.

CHAPTER 7: MUSINGS

musings

noun. Thoughtful reflections or contemplations, often of a somewhat introspective or philosophical nature.

—

Somewhere along the way, in the early days of working on this book, it started to do what a lot of created things do: take on a life of its own. Brainstorming ideas, writing, deleting, and rewriting eventually birthed the previous six chapters. Those chapters revealed themselves in an order that made sense to us, with a language and syntax we thought best. We strove to be as helpful and thorough (and concise) to as many readers as possible. This last chapter is no different – well, at least, no different in that our goal is to help. Maybe we'll take a few more chances, inject some personal opinions, perhaps even jest in our exploration of interesting and tough topics such as cynicism, self-reflection, competition, the ⅔ rule, post-gig depression, and even front lounge flatulence. Okay, maybe we'll skip that last one. Without further ado, we hope you enjoy our musings on the music industry.

—

"The Hang" (Interpersonal Skills) - Obviously the musician's profession is a precarious one. Luck, hard work, age, circumstance, nepotism, emotional awareness and composure, abilities, and intellect all play a part in your successes. The unique personalities, atypical schedule, and sometimes overall lack of structure in the music business can become a proverbial minefield. So with all of that in mind, one of the most important things you can do is develop strong interpersonal skills. As a hired musician, your income is going to come from another person, and how you interact with them can heavily affect your earning potential. Imagine seriously offending a bandleader because you said something inappropriate or rude. Are they likely to put you at the top of their call list? Spoiler alert: no. You're there to provide a service and be paid for that service. And no one wants to work with someone who is difficult to be around.

Employers don't have the time, resources, or patience to provide social training. They likely won't even know (or care) why you're acting the way you are; they'll just know that they would rather not hire you again. Self-reflection, which we'll talk more about later, is an important exercise; you'll need it to interact gracefully with your fellow musicians. Be kind and courteous, show up on time, and remember to treat others how you would like to be treated.

You will inevitably come across some interesting characters in our industry, to say the least. Musicians and artists can sometimes be carefree, impulsive, abstract, free-thinking, and not-so-pragmatic. All of these aren't necessarily bad traits, but combining a quirky business with quirky people on a bus or in a studio can sometimes create conflict and awkward situations. It can also test your patience at times. Remember to take a deep breath and consider the fact that it's not always about you. Sometimes people can be oblivious to the impact they have on others. As much as you can, make a concerted effort to control your emotions and focus on yourself. The rest is out of your control.

Our two cents: Even if you're a bit more reserved, try to spend at least some extra time with your co-workers when and if you can. This is really important in the early stages of working with new people. We're all communal creatures to an extent, and allowing others to get to know us will build rapport; you might even meet a lifelong friend like we did! *Aww...*

"The Hands" (Ability) - Just as any good artist knows which brush and what colors to use to paint a sunset, a musician should have the same ability to paint a picture with their instrument or voice. Whether you're playing country, classical, avant-garde jazz, or even polka, the importance of facility on your instrument cannot be overstated. You have to be able to play well. Now, knowing what's genre-appropriate and when (and when not) to play is another matter entirely. Developing this knowledge will take time, experience, and maturity.

To use an obvious and extreme example, you probably won't be improvising blues licks on a baroque piece or adding slap bass to a country ballad. Or consider the more practical example of using modal mixture to insert a minor pentatonic lick over a major chord. There are times when taste beats technique; just because you have access to all kinds of chops doesn't mean you always have to use them. You can gain maturity in your playing in a few different ways, including:

- Transcribing - Whether directly to your instrument or through notation, transcribing can be a good way to learn what works in a song. By doing this, you have excellent examples that can be learned from, copied, and assimilated into your own playing.
- Jam Sessions - Jams will give you a chance to stretch and experiment musically. There's a freedom and

growth that accompanies going through your own trial and error.
- Studio Work - In this format, producers, artists, and fellow musicians will provide immediate feedback for what works and what doesn't work regarding parts. There's also a fair amount of pressure in this environment, which makes for a great training ground.
- Ask - Consult a teacher, mentor, or other experienced musicians about what constitutes good taste as a player.

These are all good ways to work on refining your skills as a musician and learning how to employ them appropriately. Together, between having "hands" and the knowledge of what to do with them, you'll find yourself turning heads and be well on your way to landing great gigs.

Our two cents: As important as it is to practice, one thing that is often overlooked is the profound impact that just LISTENING has on you as a musician. Find your favorite songs (any and all genres) and obsess over them. Sit in your favorite recliner with headphones, drive around town with the volume cranked, or even have them on in the background while you cook. What you listen to will eventually show up in your playing and become part of your musical DNA.

To Move or Not to Move - If you have "the hang" and "the hands" under control but your career is still in the toilet, you're probably wondering what you're doing wrong. As the first and only human inhabitant of Antarctica, maaaaybe it's time to consider moving somewhere with a bigger music scene. If your city doesn't even have one, how are you going to make it as a musician? Smaller cities can have somewhat of a local music scene, but it's rare to see them have as many opportunities as the big three:

Nashville, New York, and Los Angeles. These are generally regarded as the main hubs for studios and touring. Occasional online viral sensations and remote tracking wizards aside, you're going to need a real and tangible music community.

Sometimes you can build a career locally and then move to a bigger city. You just have to decide if what you're leaving behind in your hometown is worth the move. Maybe you're single and want to try your hand at a new experience, or maybe you're happy where you are and choose to make the most of your local scene. If moving is not an option for you, don't discount the idea of traveling to a bigger city to network and gig on occasion. If you're ambitious enough, it's possible to have your cake and eat it too.

Our two cents: The world has become more connected thanks to the internet, and with it come plenty of opportunities to further your career. However, having face-to-face meetings that establish personal relationships and being able to be on "the scene" any night of the week is going to give you an advantage.

Make Getting Paid Your Forte - Some things we all run into early on and end up dealing with fairly regularly are setting rates, collecting money that is owed to you, and negotiating raises. We touched on these in our chapter about money, but wanted to delve a little deeper into them here.

Setting Rates

There are really no standard rates outside of ones listed by the musicians' unions. For the most part, the market you're in will set itself based on different factors, and rates can vary greatly. Each of us has an amount that we'd like (and need) to make, so what's "worth it" will depend on each person and their needs. This will also change over time based on family, health, debt, and goals. Find an amount that works for you based on research. Ask musicians in your city, Google, or check with your local musicians' union. You may be surprised to find that many rates in larger markets will actually give you a pretty decent idea of what to expect. That being said, some situations will exceed expectations and some will fall short, so use those rates as loose guidelines. Keep in mind that what constitutes opportunity for some people might be worthless to others. And remember, as with many things in this business, you'll benefit greatly from personal research and seeking advice from your fellow musicians.

Collecting

Most businesses have a collections department. In our case, other than unions, performance rights organizations (also known as PROs), and a select few independent companies, the burden of collection falls on us as musicians. This is especially true as an early-career independent contractor. Follow-up emails and texts will be your best friends: "As per my last email..." and "Friendly reminder..." are two particularly comical and passive-aggressive favorites. Every now and then you'll run into problems, and someone will owe you money for a long period of time. You'll have to decide if an invoice reminder, mediation, or small claims court is the path forward. Keep good records and carefully weigh the financial burden and time commitment that resolution efforts might take. Sometimes it might be better to just cut your losses and move on. Although this can be an unfortunate reality, over time you'll learn how to avoid shady situations and characters, and eventually (hopefully) only work for reputable people.

Negotiating Raises

Asking for a raise can be a nuanced process. Timing, tone, and emotion are at least some of the elements often at play here. Understanding the value you are (or aren't) bringing to someone before discussing the subject will enable you to have self-confidence and articulate why a raise is warranted. Some organizations actually have raises automatically built in. (Wow, that makes it easy.) Others award them yearly or on special occasions, some rarely, and a few never give them out. There are a few different ways you can go about asking for a raise: You can either ask directly or indirectly. A direct approach would be using a mediator – such as a bandleader, tour manager, or day-to-day manager. Indirectly, one approach is to create scarcity (make yourself less available) to increase your perceived value – AKA "Due to high demand ... either pay me right or get left!"

Our two cents: There may be times in the early days when you're just figuring it out as you go. Some gigs may not pay you promptly, fairly, or even at all. There's gonna be a club owner that stiffs you, or a band you have to quit because the pay sucks. It's all part of "paying dues," but don't discount the lessons and connections you'll gain through these experiences. Eventually, you'll leave those early challenges in the dust and find yourself in a place where the pay matches the opportunity.

Two Out of Three Ain't Bad - A common principle musicians use when determining whether or not they want to accept a gig is the ⅔ rule. The basic premise is that you want to have at least two of the following things to make the gig worth doing:

1. Good pay.
2. Good people.
3. Good music.

"Good" is the operative and subjective word here obviously, and it will take time to define what good means to you. Sometimes you'll get lucky and land a gig that has all three (good pay, people, and music). Cherish those, as this doesn't always happen.

Our two cents: Most of us have done gigs with only one redeeming quality, and those can be a bit soul-sucking. You can stick it out for a while if the bread is good enough, but eventually you'll want to keep your ears open for a new opportunity. You'll find that the soul-sucking ones start to have a negative impact on other areas of your life, namely your mood, energy level, satisfaction, and peace of mind.

Road Dogs vs. Studio Cats - These are two of the most commonly known animals in the music kingdom. Some musicians resonate with one more than the other. Finding out which of them (or a combination of both) aligns with your goals will help you sharpen the skills you need to pay the bills. This can change over time, but it's good to think about what makes sense in the immediate future. You'll have to decide if touring is for you – some people love it and some hate it. You may start out with stars in your eyes only to realize you'd rather be planting peppers in your garden than snackin' on airport sandwiches during layovers. Some musicians even spend their earlier years on the road and transition to being full-time studio players when the allure of the road fades. Finding your place on the spectrum of studio to stage will take time, but as with many great things, this has a way of working itself out.

Let's walk through some scenarios that will paint a picture of the dynamics between live and studio work. There are many variables in the music business that can dictate why a person might prefer to stay closer to home vs. traveling the world, or vice versa.

Scenario 1: Guy with a wife and four kids doesn't want some of the challenges that come with travel, such as being gone from home for weeks at a time, missing football games and dance recitals, and not being able to sleep in his own bed. A studio musician's career may suit this person better than life on the road.

Scenario 2: Small town girl (living in a lonely world) is single and has the desire to travel. She's in her mid-20s and wants to land an international tour that may keep her gone for weeks at a time. With little to no responsibilities back home, she may want to pursue a career in live performance.

Scenario 3: Touring guy loves to record in the studio, but has accepted a gig with a ton of tour dates, and this will take him away from home for weeks, maybe even months at a time. It's still possible for him to participate in some session work, but with such a busy touring schedule, recording sessions will be few and far between.

Scenario 4: Studio guy enjoys the road occasionally, but recording is his bread and butter. The phone rings off the hook daily from producers and remote clients. He happens to have a weekend open and an A-list artist books him for a TV date. While gigs like this are fun once in a blue moon, the studio will always come first for this guy.

These are four somewhat common scenarios, but the possibilities are virtually endless. Whether you're recording under the AC in sweatpants or shredding under an afternoon sun at a festival, you'll need to find what best fits your lifestyle and skill set.

Our two cents: Life doesn't always go your way, and compromise isn't always the end of the world. We all want to check certain boxes that we have for our careers. The saying "bloom where you are planted" is very relevant here. If you've dreamed of headlining Red Rocks but find yourself at Ocean Way in Studio A, don't be afraid to run with it! Stay true to the aspirations of your heart, but remember any day you get to play music for a living is a great day, no matter the setting.

Regret, Burnout, and Cynicism - Lions and tigers and bears, indeed! Almost everyone experiences at least one of these to some degree during their career, but through awareness and effort they can be minimized and hopefully avoided. Let's chat about what these three are, as well as some steps you can take to combat them.

Regret

We all know the expressions: "If I knew then what I know now," "hindsight's 20/20," "live and learn." They're just as apropos for the music biz as they are for anything else in life. We all look back and see things we could've done differently. These disappointments are okay as long as you learn from them, adapt, and don't allow them to define you. Part of the inspiration for this book was the desire to encourage musicians and help them guard against regret – specifically, the regret of not trying hard enough or even not trying at all.

Steps to take:
- Stay positive and don't let others discourage you. It's likely you will have some doubters, but don't let them

get in your head.
- Try. A surefire way to have regrets is to stay on the sidelines and never attempt anything due to a fear of failure. Life is short. Go for it!
- Have long-term goals in mind and make sure your career is progressing. Take the steps necessary to ensure this, even if that means leaving your current gig.
- Save when the money is flowing in.
- Continually work hard and learn new skills.
- Work a part-time job with flexible hours or teach on the side until the right full-time opportunity comes up.
- Be versatile and adaptable.
- Invest your money (stocks, real estate, retirement) early and frequently.
- Schedule intentional time for friends and family when you do have time off.
- Network often and treat everyone with kindness.

These are just a few tips on how to mitigate the sting of regret. Focus on your goals and how to attain them, keeping in mind that no one can predict the future and you can't turn back time to change the past. Ignore the naysayers and focus on what lies ahead. We can only plan for the life we'd like to have, try our best to attain it, and learn from our mistakes.

Burnout

Gigging is tough work, there's no way around it. With it come stress and fatigue. Stress and fatigue over prolonged periods of time lead to burnout, and that's a terrible state of existence for anyone. Joy and enjoyment disappear, sickness can creep in, and you'll eventually feel detached and want to quit your job altogether. And what kind of book would this be if we didn't help you avoid that?!

Steps to take:
- Rest ... literally. Get good sleep as often as you can. This will allow your mind and body to adequately recover.
- Take a few days off. It's easy to forget to do this, but most of us need at least some down time.
- Set healthy boundaries. Don't allow those work texts and emails to run your life. People can inadvertently become vampires with all of your time if you let them.
- Learn to say no. Sometimes this is hard to do in our industry, but if you have the luxury of doing so, take advantage of it when you can.
- Be mindful of your workload capacity and improve your time management skills. Don't take on more than you can handle and do a poor job because of it. Also, try not to wait until the last minute to meet deadlines for tasks like learning songs, charting tunes, or delivering remote tracks.
- Find a hobby. It doesn't have to be anything cumbersome or time-consuming, but even something small can greatly benefit your mental health.
- Prioritize uninterrupted time with family and/or friends (this is great for combating both regret and burnout).

Monetizing your skills in the aural world can be tough, and the toll it takes can be just as taxing on your mental health as it is on your physical health. Remember to be mindful of both by resting, engaging in hobbies, and enjoying life between gigs.

Cynicism

What are some words that come to mind when you think of a cynical musician? Jaded? Resentful? Bitter? Apathetic? These are definitely feelings none of us aspire to have, but everyone runs the risk of experiencing them to varying degrees at some point. Nestled somewhere between hopeless and idealistic lies the truth of the matter: that the precepts and tips in this book (hard work, kindness, tenacity, etc.) will guide and give you the best chance of success. The path toward that goal may be overgrown or dark and treacherous, but it's there nonetheless.

Steps to take:

- Think positively and don't let other people's opinions keep you from listening to your own heart and intuition. You will know what is best for you – someone else won't necessarily. Keep your head up, believe in yourself, and press on.
- Set lofty goals, but make sure they're attainable. Psychologically, it's better to knock out manageable goals than to overshoot and become discouraged.
- Don't believe or act as though you're entitled to anything. Not everyone gets everything they want in exactly the way they want it. Success is built on hard work *and* good fortune, and you aren't in control of the latter. Stay humble and accept reality on its terms, not yours.
- Don't think that your journey or destination has to look exactly like someone else's. Life is vast and you're an individual, making it likely that your path will be different from theirs.
- Realize that having and maintaining a career in music is tough and unconventional. Looking at it through the same lens as other fields might not be a good idea. You can compare and contrast, but don't expect them to be exactly the same. Oftentimes it takes a little longer to find your niche and monetize in a creative field than it does in a typical one.
- Stay flexible and adaptable, and learn new skills as needed. This will allow you to keep up with market

demands and increase your employment opportunities.
- Find peace in doing something else if a career in music doesn't pan out or just isn't for you. Keeping music as a creative outlet, hobby, or for personal enjoyment as a listener are all amazing ways you can still be involved. Other jobs may even free you up financially so you can finish that album you've been wanting to record. This would be much better than coating your life with resentment and negativity. And remember, your self-worth isn't defined by what you do.
- Just because your medieval folk rock band doesn't headline Wembley next year doesn't mean you have to hate the world.

Our two cents: It's easy to sympathize or empathize with a jaded viewpoint when you consider the disparity between those who make it and those who don't. As we've established, this business is tough. But negative energy is contagious. You have to decide whether or not you're going to fall prey to its influence or keep pushing onward in optimism. Choosing to believe that there is a path forward doesn't mean you aren't acknowledging that it's difficult or that you're completely ignoring reality; you're just choosing to persist despite these facts. Remember, "the sun'll come out tomorrow."

THE EXISTENCE OF A BRIDGE IN THE FIRST PLACE IMPLIES THAT YOU WILL BE CROSSING IT. WHY NOT STRENGTHEN AND REINFORCE IT?

Quitting, Moving On, and Retiring - Everyone eventually reaches a point in their career when they know it's time to say adios, sayonara, and peace out to a gig. It's likely to happen several times on your way to greener pastures; sometimes you just gotta moooove on (we're sorry). Whether that means quitting, moving on, or even retiring, let's explore the nuances of saying goodbye.

Quitting

There may come a time when you have to quit a gig. Nothing lasts forever, and some jobs will be stepping stones to other (perhaps better) opportunities. Knowing when and how to "exit the stage" can be a bit of an art form. We obviously know not to burn bridges, but the existence of a bridge in the first place implies that you will be crossing it. Why not strengthen and reinforce it? If the time has come to say goodbye, take the bandleader out to lunch to show appreciation or send a thank you card to the artist; little gestures like that can go a long way.

Now, all of that's assuming the gig you're leaving is at least tolerable and healthy. If a situation is toxic or stagnant and you feel like it's time to move on, maybe it is; only you will know when that time comes. When it does, you will have to summon the courage to do what needs to be done and have some tact about the situation. Try to give as much notice as you can to help make the transition smoother for your current employer. Leaving a situation on bad terms will almost always come back to haunt you in a business where reputation is everything. It's not as big of a world as you may think, and you never know when you may run into familiar faces down the road.

There may come a time when you simply just *want* to quit a gig. Whether you're being micromanaged or experiencing interpersonal conflict, everyone hits their limit eventually. Staying in a negative situation can open you up to the dangers of "quiet quitting." Quiet quitting is basically putting in the bare minimum amount of effort to keep your job, without going the extra mile for your employer. Both parties can tolerate this for a while, but it will eventually create resentment within your circle (band members, bandleader, boss, etc.).

Quitting because you have to or just because you've become complacent is never easy, but sometimes it's necessary in the long run.

Moving On

Your career will be composed of both opportunities and decisions. Projects and bands will likely come and go many times over, and it's your job to navigate your ship through a sea of pitfalls and potential. If an offer from another organization is made, it's up to you to decide whether the opportunity is enticing enough to jump ship. Maritime quips aside, this is an important issue that we'd like to dedicate a little bit of time to.

Obviously, if an opportunity is likely to improve your life drastically, the decision will all but make itself. A substantial pay increase, much better accommodations, more longevity – these are all good reasons to consider moving on. On the other hand, something that's more of a lateral career move may not always be the best course of action. Stepping sideways may ultimately be a waste of time and energy if you already have a good thing going. Weigh the pros and cons and know what your deal-breakers are because you may unintentionally jump from the frying pan into the fire.

Consider this scenario: A new gig offer comes in and it's going to put you in a better position financially, but it will also have you out on the road 300 days a year. Your current gig pays a little less, but you have much more time off to pursue other aspects of your career, and you're more available to spend free time with family and friends than you would be if you take the new gig. What's going to work better for you? Decide what that is and act accordingly.

Retiring

There comes a time in each musician's life when the tour bus rides and album deadlines come to a halt. Retiring doesn't mean that you have to stop playing music; on the contrary, you may find yourself playing more than ever. A famous example of this is cellist Pablo Casals. Pablo performed and practiced well into his 90s, and even conducted a symphony at the age of 96. On the other hand, there are variables as we get older that play into our decision to slow down later in our careers, such as health challenges and changing interests. This isn't always an option if you haven't been financially vigilant throughout your career, though. Try your best to educate yourself on the world of saving and investing so you'll have the option when the time comes.

Our two cents: One thing that sets the career of a musician apart from other career tracks is the fact that it's something you are most likely going to be extremely passionate about – otherwise, why pursue something so daunting? Sometimes, with that passion come fear and high levels of emotion regarding big gig decisions. Also, the friend/co-worker dynamic can get complicated. All of this can make quitting, moving on, or even retiring feel like the end of the world. Change is never easy, especially when you become super close on a tour bus or in a studio with friends who eventually start to feel more like family. But try to keep things in perspective, and remember at the end of the day, this is a business.

FOMO, Jealousy, and Anger - Down the rabbit hole we go. This triad can lead to general feelings of dissatisfaction with your accomplishments as well as relational fallout. And it won't be doing you any favors in terms of getting hired. If you start to feel like we're straying off the beaten path in this section, it's because we are. This rabbit hole ain't a wonderland – it's a warzone of emotions.

FOMO

In this digital world where social media is ever at our fingertips, it's easy to compare our careers to those of others. This can lead to a fear of missing out on the action. Everyone's career will look a little different, and journeys will vary. So don't hyperfixate on what someone else is doing and rob yourself of joy. Remember that social media is not real life, and just because you're not playing a huge festival on the beach today doesn't mean you shouldn't be grateful for what you have accomplished.

DON'T HYPERFIXATE ON WHAT SOMEONE ELSE IS DOING AND ROB YOURSELF OF JOY.

Jealousy

Like many other negative emotions, jealousy usually only harms the person feeling it, and the root of it is often frustration with oneself. Recognize, define, and acknowledge the deeper feelings, and then repurpose that energy as motivation and make yourself better. Don't allow insecurity based on comparison to destroy your drive. Celebrate when others succeed and be at peace knowing that you will have your own victories.

Anger

Sometimes shows and sessions can turn into high-pressure situations. When they arise, you'll need to be able to control your emotions. Ideally, you will be the calm one in the room and part of the solution to the stress.

Angry outbursts shouldn't be your go-to when frustration strikes. Just because you're having a bad day doesn't mean you should bring others down or do something you might later regret. Pause for a moment and think of some stressful situations in the past. How did you handle them, and is there anything you could've done better? If anger is a recurring theme in your life or you're prone to extremes in this area, try to develop some healthy coping skills. Do some independent research or consult a professional in this field who can help equip you with tools to be more in control of yourself.

Our two cents: If you're experiencing these feelings, take heart – that's part of being human. Just try to keep them in check, make peace with where you are in your career, and find acceptance in your own skin. Also, show grace if you encounter someone else's jealousy and try to help them if you can.

Post-Gig Depression, Self-Reflection, and Seeking Help - When you began reading this book, post-gig depression probably wasn't on your bingo card. While everyone wants to excel at their job, you can't do that if you don't guard your mental health. We felt the need to include the following subjects based on things we have encountered on our journeys. Let's give each of them their moment in the sun to discover how we can handle them appropriately.

Post-Gig Depression

After the last note decays and the tour bus rolls to a stop, you may eventually find yourself missing the thrill of performing. Once you've had time to readjust to "real" life and get back into a normal routine, you might find that post-gig depression tries to creep in. Give yourself time to feel and process your emotions, but don't invite negativity in to stay. You'll have to make sure you don't fall into bad habits while trying to replace a performance high. Surround yourself with family if you have them, and don't hesitate to reach out to friends if you're feeling low. Dive into those hobbies you've set aside and embrace each new season; there won't always be screaming fans and soaring guitar solos.

While this applies primarily to performing live, each music job can have its own version of post-gig depression. Studio musicians might experience these feelings if the phone stops ringing for sessions. Maybe some new hot-shot drummer starts getting all the calls, or your producer contact retires. Whatever the case may be, the feeling of change from the ups and downs of a rollercoaster career can affect us all in difficult ways. That's why working out, having hobbies or side hustles, and spending time with loved ones can be so helpful. If you stay active and engaged, you'll have less time to focus on the negative.

Self-Reflection

Let's start with the man in the mirror. Depending on how you're wired, you may find self-reflection difficult. While some people have the advantage of being naturally introspective, others have to make a more concerted effort.

If you find yourself unable to get or keep gigs, it can be helpful to ask yourself some tough questions to find out if *you* are the problem. Take a moment to reflect on your actions and how they've impacted you and those around you. Ask yourself the following questions:

- How do people perceive me?
- Would I hire myself based on my personality and habits?
- Do I bring up awkward subjects at the wrong time, or am I rude?
- Do I come across as harsh or demanding?
- Am I anger-prone or do I get defensive when someone is giving me feedback?
- Is there an underlying reason why my last bandleader hasn't called me for another gig?

If you answer each question honestly and allow yourself to reflect on how you can improve, great things can happen. Even though we aren't always the problem, a little self-reflection never hurt nobody!

Seeking Help

Of all the investments you can make, seeking help through counseling or therapy might be the least considered and the most important. Life's full of stressors both inside and outside of music, and we all have times in our lives when we need help. What that looks like will be different for everyone, but the important thing is that you recognize when you need help and then act on it.

Here are a few positive actions that you can take:

- Find a therapist or counselor.
- Read self-help books.
- Find and pursue a higher power.
- Join support groups.

- Spend time with trusted friends and mentors.

Also, the importance of sleep, diet, and exercise should not be discounted when it comes to the role they play in mental health. You won't be able to be the best version of you if you're struggling inside, so take care of yourself. You'll be glad you did.

Our two cents: Your gut will tell you when something is wrong. Listen to it. We all have moments in life that necessitate help, and everyone needs someone or something to lift their spirits when sadness comes knocking. Turn to the things and people that will actually deliver the goods. At the end of the day, not everyone will have your best interests at heart, but seek out those who will.

Final Thoughts: We feel compelled to remind you that neither of us have PhDs in psychology, sociology, or anything for that matter. We're just two musicians who want to bring awareness to some subjects that might not be discussed often, and see people manage their mental health better. Everyone would do well to make it more of a priority, and a little self-reflection can do you some good.

ENCORE

So you made it to the end. NICE! Our hope is that everyone from the guitar shredder to the bebop drummer can take something with them from this book. Everything we shared was done with the intent to inform and to shine a light on areas of your career that are within your control. The advice and actions you take are entirely up to you, and in some situations, there is no right or wrong answer. We've both experienced the highs and lows that come with being a musician, and at times have even failed to take our own advice. Rather than beat ourselves up about this, we've done our best to channel it into our careers and ultimately, into this survival guide.

Gone are the days of limited options when it comes to making a living as a hired musician. With the advent of new technologies, it's become easier than ever to get creative while marketing your skills and networking. In the music business, no person is an island. In the same way an artist grows a fan base, a musician should grow their network of people who believe in them. Those people are going to recommend you for jobs and help build your career. Also, remember to have faith in yourself first; this will persuade others to do the same.

We discussed self-confidence, kindness, skill, frugality, and so many other invaluable traits in this book. Some of them will take time to develop, but all will help you get and keep gigs. Rome wasn't built in a day, and the idea of an overnight sensation is a stretch. Every successful musician you idolize was most likely grinding backstage before they ever stepped foot into the limelight. So don't expect to go straight from your grandma's garage to Madison Square Garden. But if these two goobers from small-town America can, so can you. Why not go for it? You might surprise yourself. We wish you all the success in the world, and happy gigging!

RESOURCE LIST

Books
- "All You Need to Know About the Music Business" by Donald S. Passman
- "How to Win Friends and Influence People" by Dale Carnegie
- "The Nashville Number System" by Chas Williams
- "Song Charting Made Easy: A Play-Along Guide to the Nashville Number System" by Jim Riley
- "The Studio Musician's Handbook" by Bobby Owsinski and Paul III
- "Think and Grow Rich" by Napoleon Hill
- "Tonal Harmony" by Stefan Kostka, Dorothy Payne, and Byron Almén
- "The Total Money Makeover: A Proven Plan for Financial Fitness" by Dave Ramsey
- "The War of Art" by Steven Pressfield

Podcasts
- I'd Hit That
- Studio Musician Academy
- The Six Figure Home Studio

Organizations
- American Federation of Musicians (AFM)
- ASCAP / BMI / SESAC (performing rights organizations)
- National Association of Music Merchants (NAMM)
- The Recording Academy

Government Resources

- Bureau of Labor Statistics (BLS)
- Library of Congress
- National Endowment for the Arts (NEA)
- U.S. Census Bureau

INDEX

adapt, 13, 30, 48, 73, 74, 76
artist, 11, 14, 19, 23, 29, 39, 78
attitude, 10, 43, 51
audition, 15, 45, 48
band, 6, 10, 15, 19, 23, 28, 44, 51
bandleader, 21, 30, 39, 61, 65, 70, 84
burnout, 54, 74
business, 11, 15, 21, 34, 39, 44, 65, 80
career, 11, 21, 36, 47, 54, 60, 76
client, 44, 72
co-workers, 10, 20, 44, 56
emotions, 18, 65, 81
employer, 11, 19, 34, 39, 48, 50, 61, 65
equipment, 13, 38, 40
etiquette, 23
experience, 27, 36, 62, 66, 68
feedback, 11, 29, 49, 67, 84
gear, 10, 13, 15, 30, 37, 44
gigs, 7, 10, 12, 15, 20, 22, 44, 57, 61, 71, 84
goals, 34, 44, 48, 55, 69, 71, 74
hang, 6, 64, 67
health, 44, 60, 69, 75, 82, 85
hobbies, 60, 75, 83
improvise, 10, 27
income, 13, 37, 45, 59, 65
industry, 13, 18, 33, 38, 45, 53
instrument, 9, 12, 30, 40, 61, 66
insurance, 38, 40
intellectual property, 36
invest, 13, 37, 59, 74, 80, 84
jam sessions, 14, 38, 66

job, 7, 10, 18, 21, 31, 38, 46, 55, 57, 60, 74, 77
lesson, 15, 19, 35, 38, 51, 57, 70
listening, 30, 46, 51, 67, 76
manager, 39, 70
mentor, 26, 31, 40, 67, 85
money, 33, 59, 68, 74
musician, 12, 19, 28, 45, 56
music theory, 27
networking, 12, 44, 62, 86
performance, 10, 26, 30, 34, 69, 83
practice, 9, 28, 31, 49, 67
producer, 6, 29, 35, 67
rates, 38, 68
reading, 10, 28, 31, 75
recording, 12, 26, 30, 34
relationships, 15, 20, 38, 44, 60, 68
residuals, 35
service, 18, 22, 29, 65
session, 10, 30, 44, 59, 66, 82
skills, 9, 12, 19, 28, 56, 64, 71, 74, 82
social media, 20, 81
stress, 30, 37, 43, 50, 74, 82
studio, 19, 23, 30, 34, 46, 67, 71
success, 11, 19, 38, 41, 45, 48, 55, 76
teach, 35, 45, 59, 74
tour, 33, 38, 59, 68, 71
tour bus, 12, 20, 46, 61, 80, 83
union, 33, 35, 68
vibe, 6, 48
writing, 14, 36, 45

ABOUT THE AUTHORS

Mat Maxwell is an acclaimed live and studio bassist living in the Nashville area. He is the current bass player for Luke Combs and has played with Ed Sheeran, Vince Gill, Chris Young, and Wanda Jackson. Besides performance and recording, Mat teaches private lessons and hosts music clinics all across the country. A wannabe connoisseur, he finds joy in a strong cup of coffee, the rich flavors of Indian cuisine, and dark meta-humor.

—

Seth Costner is a gifted pianist, vocalist, and songwriter who has worked professionally as a sideman to many artists including Chris Young, Luke Combs, Lauren Alaina, The Drifters, The Swon Brothers and many more. He has appeared on numerous television programs such as The Today Show, Good Morning America, American Idol, the CMAs and the ACMs, among others. He hails from Gadsden, Alabama, is a graduate of Belmont University's prestigious School of Music and currently resides in Nashville, Tennessee. He has been known to wear his pajamas into Walmart at any time of day.

ACKNOWLEDGEMENTS

From Mat:
I had zero clue how to be a professional musician before meeting a teacher named Russ Head. Through his encouragement and guidance, along with the love and support of my friends and family, I've been able to make my way in this interesting and challenging career field. I'm forever grateful to them. Special thanks to my dad for spending money he didn't have to buy me my first bass guitar.

This book wouldn't have been possible without Seth Costner. He's easily one of the sharpest and most talented musicians I've ever met. I'm thankful to call him my friend and co-author. Love ya, pal.

From Seth:
I'd like to start off by thanking God for the gift of music. Also, I would not have been able to live out my dreams as a musician without the support of my parents – thank you Mom and Dad. Thanks to my Aunt Jan for teaching me my first notes on the piano and to my brother and sisters for always being there and keeping me grounded (ha!). I am thankful for every teacher throughout the years who invested in me and encouraged me to pursue this passion. To everyone who has ever allowed me to be part of their band, recording session, or musical project of any kind, THANK YOU! To the readers of this book, I appreciate your interest in our experiences in the music business. Through all of its ups and downs, I wouldn't change a thing.

Last, but certainly not least, thank you to my co-author

(and best buddy) Mat. Writing this book with you has been an amazing journey. You're one of the most talented people I've ever met, and it has truly been an honor. Love you dude. Now let's go get some Chipotle!

Special thanks:
Special thanks to Kara Coleman Fields for all the hours spent editing and formatting this book. Thanks to Adam "Tico" Hernandez for creating art through his graphic design work to communicate our vision.

Made in the USA
Columbia, SC
14 December 2024

49340790R00052